Circling Back To Jesus

30- Day Prayer Devotional

Circling Back To Jesus

30- Day Prayer Devotional

Jacquelin Maize

Copyright © 2023 Jacquelin Maize

Published by Living Water Book Publishing House

Livingwaterbooks.org

Print Book Edition 2023

Paperback - ISBN 979-8-8689-8251-4

Cover Design - Living Water Books

All rights reserved. This book is protected by the copyright laws of the United States of America. This book may not be copied or reprinted for commercial gain or profit. Any portion thereof may not be reproduced or used in any manner whatsoever without the express written permission of Jacquelin Maize except for the use of brief quotations in a book review or occasional page copying for personal or group study is also allowed and encouraged.

Please note that Living Water Books capitalizes specific
pronouns to scripture that refers to the Father, Son, and Holy
Spirit and may differ from some publishers' styles

Graphics, Art, and Designs Living Water Books

Dedication

I would like to dedicate my first book, Circling Back to Jesus, to my best friend and husband, Martin O, Maize Sr., who has been my biggest fan and encourager through this journey. Although I have always used some type of journaling throughout most of my saved life, it was Martin who insisted that I consider compiling some of the writings into a book.

Long before he became my husband Martin saw spiritual characteristics in me and decided to invest some of his precious time tutoring and teaching me on how to study the Bible. I later inherited several biblical commentaries from my dear departed friend, Jacquelyn Jones, and these books helped me to understand the scriptures even better.

However, it was watching Martin's enthusiasm in studying the word, that I begin to find that same joy in deciphering scriptures and breaking down certain words contained in the scriptures. He would tell me to always remember the law of first mentioning of a certain word in order to have a clear understanding of how the word is being used in a particular scripture.

Acknowledgements

I would like to acknowledge a wonderful God-fearing couple, Charles and LaDeidre Maris, the founders of Living Water Books Christian Publishing Company.

This gifted family unit has worked diligently with me to bring everything together in order to publish my first devotional book. To have someone take a bunch of loose papers, see my vision, and then perform all the necessary steps including the hard work of editing and proofreading my writing to end up with such a beautiful design of my book, I am most grateful.

Thank you for your patience and your prayers for my success, which has allowed me to envision and dream of my next book. May God continue to bless each of you and your publishing business.

Table Of Contents

Dedication ... 5

Acknowledgment ... 6

Introduction ... 9

Day 1 Lord, Refresh Me ... 11

Day 2 Lord, Heal Me ... 15

Day 3 Lord, Deliver Me ... 19

Day 4 Lord, I Am A New Creation ... 23

Day 5 Lord, Replace The Loneliness ... 27

Day 6 Lord, I Am Waiting for You ... 31

Day 7 Lord, Increase My Faith ... 35

Day 8 Lord, Deliver Me From Carnality ... 39

Day 9 Lord, I Desire To Grow Spiritually ... 43

Day 10 Lord, I Am Feeling Dissatisfied ... 47

Day 11 Lord, Give Me Your Grace ... 51

Day 12 Lord, Mold Me ... 55

Day 13 Lord, Clear My Mind ... 59

Day 14 Lord, Bring My Family Together ... 63

Day 15 Lord, I Am Feeling Alone ... 67

Day 16 Lord, I'm Thankful For Grace ... 71

Day 17 Lord, I Am Feeling Rejected ... 75

Day 18 Lord, My World Feels Upside Down ... 79

Table Of Contents

Day 19 Lord, These Are Dangerous Times 83

Day 20 Lord, Let My Light Shine 87

Day 21 Lord, Lead Me 91

Day 22 Lord, Deliver Me From Enemies 95

Day 23 Lord, Make Me Whole 99

Day 24 Lord, Send Your Word To Heal 103

Day 25 Lord, Help Me To Obey 107

Day 26 Lord, Here We Go Again 111

Day 27 Lord, Remember My Children 115

Day 28 Lord, You're My Strength and Shield 119

Day 29 Lord, I need Refreshing 123

Day 30 Lord, I will Pray Without Ceasing 127

About The Author 131

Publisher 132

Introduction

Once again, I must give credit to whom it is due. Around May 2021, when the COVID pandemic was in high gear, my husband said, "The Lord instructed me to tell you to start a LIVE streaming prayer time on Facebook." I immediately said, "No, why would He (the Lord) tell me to do something that you should be doing?" Nevertheless, I stopped allowing my emotions and fears to sidetrack me, and I trusted my husband to have heard from God. Therefore, the 30-minute prayer time with Jacquelin Maize was created on the Facebook pages of Martin and Jacquelin Maize. Each Sunday at 8:30 am CST we posted a spiritual-political prayer.

It was from these weekly Facebook prayers that the idea of my devotional prayer was birthed. I started with a desire to write a 365-day devotional; however, that idea quickly dissolved. I soon realized that I was biting off more than I could chew. I was trying to run before I could walk. My excessively grand and/or ambitious desire was not currently in God's plans. I had become so overwhelmed that I just stopped writing altogether.

The simple prayers I prayed each morning about my struggles, disappointments, wishes, and desires died an unnecessary death. God , stirred me up again and one day I found myself at Best Buy buying a new computer and printer in preparation to start writing again. Only, this time I felt more purpose-driven. I felt the need to bless someone else with a daily prayer devotional; just one month of prayers, a 30-day devotional. The idea led me to my title of the devotional, *Circling Back to Jesus*. The Lord gave me a second chance and I knew I needed to circle back around and do what the Lord put in my spirit.

You will find prayers of hurt, loss, pain, peace, hope, and grace. Please know that my deepest prayer is that each of you will personally find Jesus in the prayers and discover how to circle back to loving yourself and Jesus.

DAY 1

LORD, REFRESH ME

Psalm 107:20; John 15:7; Proverbs 4:20-22

A new beginning is considered as an opportunity to start over yet, it is at this time that I feel so alone. I am at the end of a phase in life where it is time to say, Lord, I need a refresher because this past year has been a whirlwind of changes and disappointments. I cannot see the positive because the negatives have been so overwhelming. Lord, help me to incline my ears unto your words. I will keep your words amid my heart and mind. Refresh me, Lord, as I refuse to let them depart from my eyes.

In your word, I find life and the health of my body comes into agreement with your word. God you have promised that your word is life and will bring healing to my spirit and physical body. Refresh me Lord, and I shall abide in you, as your promises abide in me. Refresh me Lord for this is a new beginning in my life and I refuse to focus on how I feel. I am planted in your word and my roots run deep. In Jesus' Name Amen, so be it!

CIRCLE BACK TO JESUS

DATE

BIBLE VERSE OF THE DAY:

MY THOUGHTS:

I AM THANKFUL FOR:

PRAYER

CIRCLE BACK TO JESUS

CIRCLE BACK TO JESUS

DAY 2

LORD, HEAL ME

Isaiah 55:11; Psalm 107:19-20; Isaiah 57:19

Lord, I pray against a year of struggles, both mentally and physically. I declare that your Word will not return to you void and shall accomplish what you set it out to do regarding me. Healing is my portion and you've sent your Word to heal me. Lord, I am crying for you to deliver me from these troubles and save me from all the distress that afflicts my body and mind. If the doctors tell me that there is no hope, help me to put my total trust in you to speak the Word over myself.

Lord, I know that I can speak and you will hear me because my voice matters to you. You are the multiplier and with every word I speak according to your will, you multiply my requests. You are not like a man, who will turn a deaf ear to my requests or ignore my cries. You don't pretend that you are listening outwardly, yet tune me out inwardly, just to get me to move on and shut up. So, I thank you, Lord. I truly thank you Lord that your Word can change my sickness into healing and bring me back to health. In Jesus' Name Amen, so be it!

CIRCLE BACK TO JESUS

DATE

BIBLE VERSE OF THE DAY:

MY THOUGHTS:

I AM THANKFUL FOR:

PRAYER

CIRCLE BACK TO JESUS

CIRCLE BACK TO JESUS

DAY 3

LORD, DELIVER ME

John 8:32, 36; I John 4:4; Proverbs 15:13; Psalm 34:18

Lord, deliver me from me. Help me to recognize my own shortcomings and how often I may neglect my relationship with you. I have been so consumed with myself that I have failed to honor you in my life. Your word tells me that when I know and accept the truth I will be made free. I want to be free in my mind, body, spirit, and soul. I want to be free to be who you have designed me to be from the foundation of my creation. I am free to walk in your grace, goodness, mercy, and most importantly, your love.

Lord, I see me. I see my broken spirit and I see the little girl who feels lost in her past. I feel sorry for myself because of the great losses I have experienced such as growing up without a father whom I lost at the age of two, and without a mother whom I lost at the age of fifteen. These losses have caused me to suffer inwardly for many years. Hereby, I am denouncing this spirit of sorrow and will allow the Holy Spirit to mend this broken heart. I decree that I am an overcomer and greater is He that is in me than he that is in this world. In Jesus' Name Amen, so be it!

CIRCLE BACK TO JESUS

DATE

BIBLE VERSE OF THE DAY:

MY THOUGHTS:

I AM THANKFUL FOR:

PRAYER

CIRCLE BACK TO JESUS

CIRCLE BACK TO JESUS

DAY 4

LORD, I AM A NEW CREATURE

**II Corinthians 5:17; Psalm 103:12; I John 2:1;
Hebrews 8:12; I John 1:9; Psalm 85:2; Isaiah 55:7**

Lord, I know your scriptures state, "Therefore, if any mankind is in Christ, he is a new creature: old things are passed away; behold, all things have become new." But what if I did not become new, what if I have remained as my old self? What if I confessed my sins, but continued in some of my sins? Am I still forgiven? Have my transgressions been removed? Are my sins covered? Lord Jesus, you are my advocate with the Father. You are faithful and just to forgive my sins, cleansing me from all unrighteousness. Therefore, I forgive myself, Lord. I will no longer hold the sins that you have forgiven against myself.

I will continue to repent and confess my sins, knowing that you Lord, are faithful and just to forgive my sins. You abundantly pardon me! I am being liberated from unrighteousness and you have promised that you will not remember my sins and iniquities, anymore. Thank you, Lord! I praise you and magnify your name. In Jesus' Name Amen, so be it!

CIRCLE BACK TO JESUS

DATE

BIBLE VERSE OF THE DAY:

MY THOUGHTS:

I AM THANKFUL FOR:

PRAYER

CIRCLE BACK TO JESUS

CIRCLE BACK TO JESUS

DAY 5

LORD, REPLACE THE LONLINESS

Isaiah 41:10; John 14:18; I Peter 5:7; Psalm 46:1; Hebrews 13:5; Isaiah 51:11

Lord, I am so tired of being alone. Please replace this loneliness that I feel with joy and strength. It is awful to feel alone while having someone to share life with. There was a time that I remember feeling this way years ago, but now that you have blessed me with a spouse, I would think that I should feel more fulfilled in life. However, the loneliness still lingers within me. I am finally realizing that the loneliness I feel is my disconnection from you, Lord, and it has nothing to do with a spouse. Lord, you promised that you would never leave me nor forsake me, but where are you, Lord? I cannot feel you and I cannot sense your presence. Lord, I do not understand why this void has filled my soul. I am trying to cast all my cares upon you because I know that you care about me. So, be my comforter, help me to know that you are with me. You are my refuge and my strength. I know if I wait on you, you will renew my strength and fill this void with your presence. When I call on you, you will answer. The sorrow and mourning shall flee away and be replaced with gladness and joy. In Jesus' Name Amen, so be it!

CIRCLE BACK TO JESUS

DATE

BIBLE VERSE OF THE DAY:

MY THOUGHTS:

I AM THANKFUL FOR:

PRAYER

CIRCLE BACK TO JESUS

CIRCLE BACK TO JESUS

DAY 6

LORD, I AM WAITING ON YOU

Psalm 27:14; 62:5; 145:15; Isaiah 40:31; Habakkuk 2:3; Hebrews 10:23

Lord, I am waiting on you and I know that I should hold on to my faith and be encouraged while I wait because you are faithful to all your promises. Lord, I already know that for You to say a thing, is for You to do it because Your word does not return unto You void; Therefore, even if it seems like I have been waiting for such a long time, I must allow my strength to be renewed as I continue to wait.

My confidence in you is strong without wavering because I have seen your work in my life. So, this is nothing new for you. You have opened Your hands and provided my deepest desires many times. I put my trust in you Lord and my soul will wait for the Lord because my expectation is from HIM. Even if my request tarry, I will wait for it because it will surely come. In Jesus' Name Amen, so be it!

CIRCLE BACK TO JESUS

DATE

BIBLE VERSE OF THE DAY:

MY THOUGHTS:

I AM THANKFUL FOR:

PRAYER

CIRCLE BACK TO JESUS

CIRCLE BACK TO JESUS

DAY 7

LORD, INCREASE MY FAITH

**Hebrews 11:1; Romans 10:17; Romans 12:3;
Hebrews 11:6; Mark 9:23; I John 5:4; I Peter 1:7**

Yes, I know faith comes from hearing God's Word and faith is the evidence of things not seen. I have heard those scriptures all my life but Lord, I am sorry that my faith seems to be turning into unbelief. I don't doubt you, God, but unfortunately, the delayed prayers I experienced caused me to think that you wouldn't come through for me. The trials of my faith are being tested, and I feel that I am failing you God because my faith should be more precious than gold to me. Yet, when my faith is tried with fire, I lose hope because things are not happening according to my timing.

God, restore my mind to the place of peace. Strengthen my hope as I delight myself in you. I don't know the timetable you had with Job, in the book of Job but I am reminded that they that wait on the Lord shall renew their strength. So, Lord, I do believe that all things are possible through you, and I trust You. In Jesus' Name Amen, so be it!

CIRCLE BACK TO JESUS

DATE

BIBLE VERSE OF THE DAY:

MY THOUGHTS:

I AM THANKFUL FOR:

PRAYER

CIRCLE BACK TO JESUS

CIRCLE BACK TO JESUS

DAY 8

LORD, DELIVER ME FROM CARNALITY

**Romans 8:6; Proverbs 14:12; I Timothy 5:6;
Romans 12:2; Philippians 2:5**

Lord, your Word speaks about how the carnal mind is death; but to be spiritually minded is life and peace. Lord, I want peace and I want to have life in abundance. Yet, I find myself succumbing to the thoughts that invade my mind and pull me into the flesh, which does not please you. Lord, so often I allow myself to fall into ways that seem to be right, but as I go deeper into those areas I realize I'm on the wrong path. Your Word lets me know that if I live in the pleasures of this world, I am yet dead while I live.

So, Lord, I have to change my mindset and allow the mind of Christ to be in me. Help me Lord, to renew my mind, so that I might display what is thy good, acceptable, and perfect will of God. In Jesus' Name Amen, so be it!

CIRCLE BACK TO JESUS

DATE

BIBLE VERSE OF THE DAY:

MY THOUGHTS:

I AM THANKFUL FOR:

PRAYER

CIRCLE BACK TO JESUS

CIRCLE BACK TO JESUS

DAY 9

LORD, I DESIRE TO GROW SPIRITUALLY

Hebrews 11:6; II Timothy 2:15; I Timothy 4:15; Hebrews 6:1; Colossians 3:16; Philippians 1:6; Colossians 1:9-11

Where do I start? How do I rekindle my relationships with you Lord? All I can do is begin with the greatest book in the world, which begins with these words, "In the beginning, God." I know that unless I believe these first four words of the Bible and believe that faith has to dominate all that I do from this day forward, I will be lost. I will not receive the reward that is set before me. Yes Lord, let me begin to diligently seek you. Let me begin to study to show myself approved unto God. Help me to rightly divide the word of truth from the false and deceptive words of unfruitful and unrighteous people.

I must begin to meditate on the word and things of God. Oh Father, let your Word dwell in me richly in all wisdom; let me not cease to pray and desire more knowledge of you. Let your love abound in me that I might walk worthy of you and be fruitful in every good work. As I increase in the knowledge of God, I am confident that he who has begun a good work in me will perform it until the day of Jesus Christ. In Jesus' Name Amen, so be it!

CIRCLE BACK TO JESUS

DATE

BIBLE VERSE OF THE DAY:

MY THOUGHTS:

I AM THANKFUL FOR:

PRAYER

CIRCLE BACK TO JESUS

CIRCLE BACK TO JESUS

DAY 10

LORD, I AM FEELING DISSATISFIED

**Psalm 34:10; Matthews 5:6; Psalm 103:1-5;
Isaiah 12:2-3; Psalm 107:9**

Oh God, I trust you! I am in pursuit of you and my soul is thirsting for you. Fill me up Lord and satisfy me with your goodness. I am thirsty for righteousness, hungry for your love, and a deep longing to be filled by you. I feel that you are far from me and you have closed your ears to my cry. I am trying hard to remember all of your blessings and benefits. I hold each time that you have healed me of diseases or forgiven my iniquities very close. I see goodness and mercies following me at all times, and I feel the grace of God daily. You have redeemed my life from destruction and covered me with your loving, kindness, and tender mercies. I will shout from the highest mountain that God is good and his mercies endure forever. "Bless the Lord, O my soul: and all that is within me, bless his holy name." In Jesus' Name Amen, so be it!

CIRCLE BACK TO JESUS

DATE

BIBLE VERSE OF THE DAY:

MY THOUGHTS:

I AM THANKFUL FOR:

PRAYER

CIRCLE BACK TO JESUS

CIRCLE BACK TO JESUS

DAY 11

LORD, GIVE ME YOUR GRACE

Proverbs 3:4; Psalm 84:11; Exodus 33:17; Job 10:12; Proverbs 8:35; Hebrews 4:16; Proverbs 10:22

Lord, I really want to experience your favor. I desire to walk upright before you and I know that you will not withhold any good thing from me. I trust you, Lord. Your grace shines upon all because you are truly no respecter of persons. "For whosoever finds ME finds life, and shall obtain favor of the Lord." Father, you know me by my name; therefore, you have promised to do whatever I ask, according to your Will, because I will always find grace in your sight. Thank you, Lord, that your blessings make me rich mentally, physically, and emotionally. So, Lord, I come to the throne of grace, boldly, because I know it is there that I will obtain your mercy, and find the grace of God in my time of need. In Jesus' Name Amen, so be it!

CIRCLE BACK TO JESUS

DATE

BIBLE VERSE OF THE DAY:

MY THOUGHTS:

I AM THANKFUL FOR:

PRAYER

CIRCLE BACK TO JESUS

CIRCLE BACK TO JESUS

DAY 12

LORD, MOLD ME

Hebrews 6:1; II Peter 3:18; I Peter 2:2, 3; II Timothy 2:15; James 1:23; Colossians 1:10; 3:16

Lord, I have walked in my own ways for far too long and I need to be made new. Make me over Lord. Mold me into the person you designed me to be from creation. I denounce a belief in only the principles of the doctrine of Christ, and I move on to seeking the perfecting Christ in my life. My life should not consist of only beliefs taught by the church and/or political parties. These beliefs do not always line up with your truth and the contents of your Word. It leads me to pursue perfection and not grace. Perfection is not what God desires from us. Help me to study your Word Lord and enable me to separate the Word of truth from the unfruitful words of man. I declare that your promises dwell within me richly and I am multiplying in you, God. Your word says that you will complete the work you started in me, so I thank you for molding me and I thank you for watching over my life. In Jesus' Name Amen, so be it!

CIRCLE BACK TO JESUS

DATE

BIBLE VERSE OF THE DAY:

MY THOUGHTS:

I AM THANKFUL FOR:

PRAYER

CIRCLE BACK TO JESUS

CIRCLE BACK TO JESUS

DAY 13

LORD, CLEAR MY MIND

Psalm 55:22; Psalm 119:165; Psalm 30:5; Psalm 147:3; Romans 8:39

Lord, I know that you did not give me the spirit of fear; but of power, love, and of a sound mind. However, I find myself struggling mentally because of the fear that tries to overpower my thoughts. Thank you, Lord, for your strength for upholding me with your right hand, and for encouraging me to, "fear not." My God, your Word states that you are not the author of confusion, but of peace; therefore, I am asking you to bind up my broken heart and the wounds that the cares of this world have inflicted upon me. The wounds bring forth confusion in the areas where I desire peace.

Oh Father, let the peace of God rest upon me. I cast my burdens upon you Lord. Please sustain me in your love as I keep my mind on you! Nothing shall separate me from the love of God, not hypocrisy, confusion, partiality, or principalities. "Great peace have they which love your law: and nothing shall offend them." I rest in the promises. In Jesus' Name Amen, so be it!

CIRCLE BACK TO JESUS

DATE

BIBLE VERSE OF THE DAY:

MY THOUGHTS:

I AM THANKFUL FOR:

PRAYER

CIRCLE BACK TO JESUS

CIRCLE BACK TO JESUS

DAY 14

LORD, BRING MY FAMILY BACK TOGETHER

James 1:19; Ephesians 4:26, 31-32; Proverbs 15:1; 16:32

Lord, help my family to unite as one. Oh God, it just seems like my family is divided, and dysfunctional both naturally and spiritually. I know you tell us to let all bitterness, wrath, anger, and evil speaking, be put away, but what happens when there is no communication just blaming, accusing, and sometimes name-calling? Lord, there is so much pain and unforgiveness in my family, and it seems that is partly due to the loss of our parents at such an early age.

Help us learn to be slow to speak, swift to listen, and allow a soft answer to replace the grievous words that stir up anger. Your word teaches us that it is okay to be angry but don't allow sin to enter into our hearts due to the anger. Lord, help my family to develop more self-control, and not allow anger to guide and direct our lives. I know that we should not hold on to grudges, or nurse hurt feelings. So Lord, help us to clear out the debris from our eyes that causes our perception to replay the negative. Your word shows us how to be kind, tenderhearted, and forgiving to one another, even as we are forgiven by Christ. In Jesus' Name Amen, so be it!

CIRCLE BACK TO JESUS

DATE

BIBLE VERSE OF THE DAY:

MY THOUGHTS:

I AM THANKFUL FOR:

PRAYER

CIRCLE BACK TO JESUS

CIRCLE BACK TO JESUS

DAY 15

LORD, I FEEL ALONE

I Corinthians 12:12-27; Galatians 6:2; Romans 14:19; Hebrews 13:1; Genesis 4:9

Lord, sometimes I feel so alone. Even with many sisters in Christ, I still feel alone. It seems that even Christians allow jealousy and envy to control their thoughts, just as the worldly do. I know the Bible states that we are many members, yet one body; however, some members act as if they do not need the other members. Lord God, are we not supposed to bear each other's burdens? I understand that support and honor should be given to all members of the body of Christ but some think some are less honorable; and are deemed unnecessary to the body of Christ.

Lord you have set every member in the body as it pleases you, so no part of the body can say to another part of the body that it is not needed. The eye cannot say to the hand, I have no need of thee: nor the head to the feet, for the body to be whole, the body needs all parts. Lord, help us to pursue what brings peace and mutual edifying, and let brotherly love continue. In Jesus' Name. Amen, so be it!

CIRCLE BACK TO JESUS

DATE

BIBLE VERSE OF THE DAY:

MY THOUGHTS:

I AM THANKFUL FOR:

PRAYER

CIRCLE BACK TO JESUS

CIRCLE BACK TO JESUS

DAY 16

LORD, I AM THANKFUL FOR YOUR GRACE

Proverbs 14:9; Psalm 23:6; Job 10:12; Psalm 16:11

Oh God, I thank you for Grace. "Fools make a mockery at sin but among the righteous there is favor." I want your favor Lord, but I know that I do not always deserve it. Your Word lets me know that you want to be searched after in order to find life and obtain favor from you.

Regardless of my being so undeserving, you are still mindful of me. You bless me, my family, and my home! Thank you for providing me with unmerited favor, and allowing your goodness and mercy to follow me all the days of my life. I thank you for granting me life and for your visitations that bring me strength, love, and joy unspeakable. Lord, I want to be in your presence, where there is fullness of joy, and at your right hand are pleasures forevermore. So, keep me, Lord, even when I do not understand why you are so faithful to me. In Jesus' Name Amen, so be it!

CIRCLE BACK TO JESUS

DATE

BIBLE VERSE OF THE DAY:

MY THOUGHTS:

I AM THANKFUL FOR:

PRAYER

CIRCLE BACK TO JESUS

CIRCLE BACK TO JESUS

DAY 17

LORD, I AM FEELING REJECTED

Luke 6:22; Isaiah 43:5; Matthew 5:44; Romans 12:19; Ephesians 4:32

Lord, why do I feel rejected and unliked by so many? What am I doing, or what am I not doing that causes so many to act as if they do not like me? Sometimes even my own family clashes with me. The Bible tells me, "Blessed are you when people hate, exclude, and revile you;" "Fear not, for I am with you; be not dismayed, for I am your God." Lord, I do not feel as if I am always right in every situation that I encounter, but even after I apologize, the situation is still unresolved and tense. I am trying to learn how to speak less, be slow to speak and quick to hear. Maybe I can help keep down confusion by just being quiet and not being so quick to let anger rest in my bosom. I should love my enemies and do good to those who hurt or hate me. This can be hard sometimes. I have to remember that I cannot seek vengeance for myself, but that God says vengeance belongs to Him. Thank you, Lord, for showing me the importance of forgiving others even as Christ has forgiven me. In Jesus' Name Amen, so be it!

CIRCLE BACK TO JESUS

DATE

BIBLE VERSE OF THE DAY:

MY THOUGHTS:

I AM THANKFUL FOR:

PRAYER

CIRCLE BACK TO JESUS

CIRCLE BACK TO JESUS

DAY 18

LORD, MY WORLD FEELS UPSIDE DOWN

II Corinthians 4:8-10; Psalm 20:2;
John 3:16; Matthew 5:14-16

Lord, our world feels like it is upside down. We are truly troubled on every side; we even feel the despair and the pains of persecution but praise God we do not feel forsaken, cast down, or destroyed. We cry out for you to help us Lord. Send help from your sanctuary, and send strength out of Zion. We need you, Lord. Please come down to see about us and do not let the enemy have victory over us. Lord, I know the depth of your love and you so loved us that you gave your only begotten son. God, you said that whosoever believes in HIM shall not perish. So, Lord, I have to believe that you will not allow the enemy and whoever he is using to destroy your people. My God, please help us to let our light shine amid the darkness and evil, because we are truly the light of the world. I declare that light will always overcome darkness, just help us to see our light and use it. In Jesus' Name Amen, so be it!

CIRCLE BACK TO JESUS

DATE

BIBLE VERSE OF THE DAY:

MY THOUGHTS:

I AM THANKFUL FOR:

PRAYER

CIRCLE BACK TO JESUS

CIRCLE BACK TO JESUS

DAY 19

LORD, I AM LIVING IN A DANGEROUS WORLD
Ephesians 4:26, 31-32; Romans 12:19; Hebrews 10:30

Lord, our world has become so dangerous. Anger and hate are controlling many people today and for whatever reason, we have reached a point in our world where kindness and love are so limited. The Bible tells us that it is all right to be angry, but not sin. However, many people are sinning in their anger, hurting others with words, and simply because anger rests in the bosoms of fools.

Lord help those of us who are being attacked and feel the need to defend ourselves. Bring to our remembrance that vengeance belongs to you, and you will judge these people according to your righteousness. My God, I pray for deliverance in the lives of those who are caught up in the cares of this world. Deliver your people from all bitterness, wrath, anger, clamor, and evil speaking. Holy Spirit, cultivate our fruit of the spirit and teach us to evolve in our love walk. Love, we give you permission to dwell within our hearts. In Jesus' Name Amen, so be it!

CIRCLE BACK TO JESUS

DATE

BIBLE VERSE OF THE DAY:

MY THOUGHTS:

I AM THANKFUL FOR:

PRAYER

CIRCLE BACK TO JESUS

CIRCLE BACK TO JESUS

DAY 20

LORD, LET MY LIGHT SHINE

Matthew 5:15-16; Psalm 119:105; Proverbs 20:24; Acts13:47

Lord, Let my light shine. Your Word teaches us to let our light so shine, that others might see our good deeds and you will be glorified in Heaven. I must admit that sometimes I find it hard to allow the light that you have put in me, to shine brightly or even at all. I believe that light enables me to see you, discern, and identify my steps. Lord, I pray that you would order my steps, right now! I feel as if I am walking in darkness stumbling through my life, and also struggling in my thoughts. How can my light shine when my life seems so dull?

Lord, I do not want darkness to overcome me, so I am reaching out to you as my sustainer and provider. Provide me with all that I need to survive this dark world and those who are bringing the darkness to life. I refuse to let my light be hidden under a bushel. I believe that my light will glow brightly and my abilities will come forth. In Jesus' Name Amen, so be it!

CIRCLE BACK TO JESUS

DATE

BIBLE VERSE OF THE DAY:

MY THOUGHTS:

I AM THANKFUL FOR:

PRAYER

CIRCLE BACK TO JESUS

CIRCLE BACK TO JESUS

DAY 21

LORD, TEACH ME HOW TO LEAD

**Psalm 119:105; 119:11; 37:23; 23:3;
Luke 1:79; Joshua 1:8; Proverbs 6:22-23;**

Lord, you're the leader of my life. "Thy word is a lamp unto my feet and a light unto my path." I tend to want to take the reins and lean to my own understanding, but I must admit that each time you bring me out of an overwhelming situation. I realize that if I hid thy word in my heart, I would not be so quick to sin against your guidance. Lord, I want you to lead me wherever I go! Whether I am asleep, or awake I want you to lead me into all truths. Your word says, "And I shall know the truth, and the truth shall make me free", And I want to be free, Lord!

I pray that you restore my soul and lead me in the paths of righteousness for your name's sake. Order my steps Lord and guide my feet into the way of peace. Give me a hunger and thirst to meditate on your law, day and night. Let your word never depart from my mouth. Therefore, this will give light to them that sit in darkness and in the shadow of death, to guide their feet into the way of peace. In Jesus' Name Amen, so be it!

CIRCLE BACK TO JESUS

DATE

BIBLE VERSE OF THE DAY:

MY THOUGHTS:

I AM THANKFUL FOR:

PRAYER

CIRCLE BACK TO JESUS

CIRCLE BACK TO JESUS

DAY 22

LORD, DELIVER ME FROM MY ENEMIES

Matthew 6:14-15; 5:12; Hebrews 10:30;
Matthew 5:44; I Peter 3:9; Romans 12:21

Lord, deliver me from my enemies. Help me to stand in my authority and speak your word against my foes as you handle those who come against me. Your word says to pray for those who speak evil against me or treat me indifferently. I should not render evil for evil or railing for railing. I will do as your word tells me. I will love my enemies, bless them that curse me, do good to them that hate me, and pray for them which despitefully use me. Lord, I do not know if I can say that I am being persecuted, because that is a strong word, but I do feel that I am being shunned by those who pretend to be my friends. However, I will not be overcome by evil, but I will overcome evil with good. I rejoice even when I don't feel like I should and I am exceedingly glad; for great is the reward that I will receive from you here on earth and in Heaven. Thank you Lord for giving me an understanding of my trials and tribulations; I especially thank you for helping me to understand that you will deliver me from the hand of my adversary. In Jesus' Name Amen, so be it!

CIRCLE BACK TO JESUS

DATE

BIBLE VERSE OF THE DAY:

MY THOUGHTS:

I AM THANKFUL FOR:

PRAYER

CIRCLE BACK TO JESUS

CIRCLE BACK TO JESUS

DAY 23

LORD, MAKE ME WHOLE

Psalm 103:3; Isaiah 53:5;
Jeremiah 17:14; 30:17; Hebrews13:8

My God, I am learning that aging and ill-health can sometimes run hand-in-hand. So, Lord help me to accept that I am blessed to have a birthday each year, even in the midst of some health issues. It would be easy to complain about how I feel each day but I am thankful for life within me. Sometimes I awake feeling great, while other times I awaken to struggles. Heal me Lord, and I shall be healed; deliver me, and I shall be delivered; for You oh lord are the only wise God. I want to hear you say, "For I will restore health unto thee, and I will heal thee. I will heal thee of your wounds.

I stand firm on the promises of healing and know that you were wounded for my transgressions, bruised for my iniquities, the chastisement of my peace was upon you Lord, and by your stripes, I am healed. Make me whole in you God so that I may continue to fulfill my purpose. Lord, you are the only one who forgives all my iniquities and can heal all the diseases that attack my body. In Jesus' Name Amen, so be it!

CIRCLE BACK TO JESUS

DATE

BIBLE VERSE OF THE DAY:

MY THOUGHTS:

I AM THANKFUL FOR:

PRAYER

CIRCLE BACK TO JESUS

CIRCLE BACK TO JESUS

DAY 24

LORD, SEND YOUR WORD TO HEAL

Isaiah 53:5; Romans 6:11; Psalm 107:20; Romans 12:1-2; Colossians 3:16

Lord Jesus, I believe you were wounded for my transgressions, bruised for my iniquities; and the chastisement of my peace was placed upon you. I am healed and it has been established. You are the Lord of my life, and when I repent I will be forgiven from sin and guilt. According to His Word, I am dead to sin and alive unto righteousness, because God has already sent His Word to heal me.

Lord, help me to present my body to you and trust your plan for me. I understand that I am transformed by the renewing of my mind, and this helps me grow in my trust and faith. Lord, I want to be filled with You. I want your word to dwell in me richly. I open my heart and permit you to enter without a reservation. I want the spiritual wealth of your healing. In Jesus' Name Amen, so be it!

CIRCLE BACK TO JESUS

DATE

BIBLE VERSE OF THE DAY:

MY THOUGHTS:

I AM THANKFUL FOR:

PRAYER

CIRCLE BACK TO JESUS

CIRCLE BACK TO JESUS

DAY 25

LORD, HELP ME TO OBEY

**John 14:15; Acts 5:29; Colossians 3: 23-25;
2 Corinthians 4:18; Psalm 100:1-4**

Oh my God, teach me to do your will; help me to walk before you in righteousness. For your word tells me that I ought to obey God rather than men. I am your child and there is nothing that will prevent me from honoring and obeying you. All that I do will be done unto the Lord, and not unto men. I do not want to focus on vain things, which cannot profit or deliver me, because they are temporal. I want to let my attention be centered on the things of God which are everlasting and eternal. Deliver me oh Lord, help me to make a joyful noise again! Help me to come before your presence with singing. I want to serve You with gladness and enter into your gates with thanksgiving, and into your courts with praise. My desire is to be thankful unto you and to bless your name. In Jesus' Name Amen, so be it!

CIRCLE BACK TO JESUS

DATE

BIBLE VERSE OF THE DAY:

MY THOUGHTS:

I AM THANKFUL FOR:

PRAYER

CIRCLE BACK TO JESUS

CIRCLE BACK TO JESUS

DAY 26

LORD, HERE WE GO AGAIN

Philippians 3:13-14; Matthew 24:6-7; Psalm 56:3; Isaiah 41:10; Proverbs 3:5-6

Lord, we need to find our way back to you, back to what really matters. Lord, help us to stay in your presence until we hear from you. Lord, we want to switch from a monologue to a dialogue, seek your face and find rest. So much hatred, so much killing, so much depression, so much worry, so much loss, and most of all so much falling away from you Lord. Help us to stay focused and to keep our eyes on you. Help us to continue to press towards the mark for the prize of your high calling God.

Oh my God, what is happening to our country, to our world? Famines, earthquakes, pestilences, plagues, wars, and viruses, are at an all-time high. Your Word tells us that such things must happen, but the end is still yet to come. Therefore, we will not fear, we will trust you, Lord. In Jesus' Name Amen, so be it!

CIRCLE BACK TO JESUS

DATE

BIBLE VERSE OF THE DAY:

MY THOUGHTS:

I AM THANKFUL FOR:

PRAYER

CIRCLE BACK TO JESUS

CIRCLE BACK TO JESUS

DAY 27

LORD, DO NOT FORGET ABOUT OUR CHILDREN

Isaiah 54:13; Proverbs 22:6; Psalm 91:11; Matthew 18:10; Proverbs 17:6; 3 John 1:4

Our children are suffering, Lord. They are being bullied and abused. Some of our children are engaged in reckless behaviors due to their outlook on life and some are even committing suicide from self-inflicted wounds and drugs. Psalm 91:11 reminds us, "For He will command His angels concerning you, to guard you in all your ways." I believe that you will watch over my children. I trust you regarding the children you have given me stewardship over!

Lord, I pray that you will open the eyes of my children and help them to see your angels surrounding them. My faith in you and the promise you have given to keep my children safe prevails in my heart. God despite the uncertainties of the world, you are my constant. I can stand on the truth and the truth shall set my family free. Though the adversary wants my children, they belong to you. Lord, do what only you can do and give me peace in my soul. I love you and I lift my children up to you. In Jesus' Name Amen, so be it!

CIRCLE BACK TO JESUS

DATE

BIBLE VERSE OF THE DAY:

MY THOUGHTS:

I AM THANKFUL FOR:

PRAYER

CIRCLE BACK TO JESUS

CIRCLE BACK TO JESUS

DAY 28

LORD, YOU ARE MY STRENGTH AND SHIELD

Psalm 28:7; 2 Thessalonians 3:3;
Psalm 27:1; Psalm 91:1-16

Lord, you are my strength and shield. My constant provider who provides all the things that keep us from dangers seen and unseen. We should not waste time and energy worrying and stressing over what the future holds, because the Word lets us know that nothing can separate us from the presence of our God. We stand in the faith.

We are sometimes troubled on every side, yet not distressed. We are perplexed but not in despair. We understand that trouble will always be a part of this world, even though trouble does not last forever. I thank God that he equips us to handle whatever we encounter, and he does not allow us to lose sight of our God and his ability to give us victory. Thank you, Lord, for being our strength and shield. In Jesus' Name Amen, so be it!

CIRCLE BACK TO JESUS

DATE

BIBLE VERSE OF THE DAY:

MY THOUGHTS:

I AM THANKFUL FOR:

PRAYER

CIRCLE BACK TO JESUS

CIRCLE BACK TO JESUS

DAY 29

LORD, I NEED REST AND REFRESHMENT

Matthew 11:28; Romans 15:32; Joshua 1:9; Psalm 94:19; Psalm 16:11; Philippians 4: 6-7; Psalm 139:7

Lord, we come into your presence seeking rest and refreshment. We marvel at the thought and wonder of being able to communicate with you. As we grow increasingly aware of your presence, we find it easier to understand your directions, which way we should go, and what decisions we should make. Lord, even though you know all about me and my shortcomings, You still love and communicate with me whenever I reach out to you.

My God, please help us to resist the urge and temptation to worry or be anxious for nothing. Because we are continually faced with things that can make us overly anxious, but we know that is only if we allow ourselves to become anxious. We know that we have to allow prayer and supplication to supersede the anxiety and to let our requests be made known to God. Lord, I am so grateful that in your presence is fullness of joy, and at your right hand, there are pleasures forevermore. In Jesus' Name Amen, so be it!

CIRCLE BACK TO JESUS

DATE

BIBLE VERSE OF THE DAY:

MY THOUGHTS:

I AM THANKFUL FOR:

PRAYER

CIRCLE BACK TO JESUS

CIRCLE BACK TO JESUS

DAY 30

LORD, I WILL PRAY WITHOUT CEASING
**1 Thessalonians 5:16-17; 1 Samuel 3:9-10; 1 John 5:14;
Mark 11:24; Psalm 143:1; Psalm 19:14**

Lord, you called me to pray without ceasing. However, I find myself lacking in the area of prayer. I admit that I do not give myself to you in prayer as I should. I find myself doing everything but praying. Help me Lord to be more disciplined and give me the mindset to seek you. You have given me the fruit of the spirit, self-control and it is so important for me to operate in this regarding us. Prayer is more than talking but also listening to you.

I surrender my mindset to you, Lord, so that when I feel anxious about any situation my confidence will be in you. I submit my petition before you and devote myself to prayer knowing that whatever I ask for in prayer, believing that I will receive it, it will be mine. I stand before you saying, Hear me oh Lord when I cry. My God, let the words of my mouth and the meditation of my heart be pleasing in your sight and my answer to your call will always be "Yes, speak Lord for thy servant heareth."
In Jesus' Name Amen, so be it!

CIRCLE BACK TO JESUS

DATE

BIBLE VERSE OF THE DAY:

MY THOUGHTS:

I AM THANKFUL FOR:

PRAYER

CIRCLE BACK TO JESUS

CIRCLE BACK TO JESUS

THE AUTHOR

JACQUELIN MAIZE

Prayer has always been a part of my life from the time I was a little girl playing with dolls and looking up in the sky..... God was there for me! My mother introduced him to me by the way she met with him to deliver all of the family into his arms. I heard her praying and her openness invited me into this intimacy! Even in moments of straying away from God, I found myself "Circling Back to Jesus" because he was and has always been my constant.

Later in life, I found myself growing in my trust in God. I found myself praying more and delivering my own family into the protection of God just like my mother. It was during a devastating divorce that my desire for God increased significantly. I was so hungry for this time of prayer with the only one who made me feel like living. God became the one I fully trusted to soothe my soul, heart, and mind. I remember having difficult moments where I didn't want to let Him in or talk to Him anymore because I was ashamed of my behavior. I thought my behavior disqualified me and I'd run away. Still, He never left me or forsook me. Yet again there I was "Circling Back To Jesus."

He was always there to pick me up and encourage me to keep putting one foot in front of the other. I now encourage you to not only read the book but "Circle Back to Jesus" Circle back and let him be the friend in your life.

Living Water Books
Living Water Books
John 7:3
CONTACT US TODAY
BUTTER BEANS & ICE CREAM

THE CHRISTIAN
PUBLISHING COMPANY
THE INTUNE HUSBAND
"He tunes into the Frequency of Heaven and reclaims territory from Hell"
Charles Maris
kindle
THE INTUNE HUSBAND
"He tunes into the Frequency of Heaven and reclaims territory from Hell"
Charles Maris
LaDeidre Maris
The Warrior Wife
kindle
LaDeidre Maris
The Warrior Wife
WEBSITE: LIVINGWATERBOOKS.ORG

www.ingramcontent.com/pod-product-compliance
Lightning Source LLC
Chambersburg PA
CBHW040807120726
48005CB00012B/1333